*I am man*

ANA MARÍA MUNAR

Ordering Information:
Ana María Munar
Copenhagen Business School
Porcelænshaven 18A
2000, Frederiksberg,
Denmark
anm.mpp@cbs.dk

*To my Kellee*
*making the world shine*

Words are both our instrument of truth and our weapon of distortion. We use them both to reveal and to conceal.[1]

Maria Popova, 2018

## FOREWORD

The idea for this book came unexpectedly and with a sense of urgency. I tried to make sense of what I was feeling at the time by writing an email to a good colleague: "These past months I have had four anecdotes with four different persons who have stated to me that "gender doesn't exist" or "I don't see gender". They don't argue for this but express it as statement. Like a "reality by enunciation". (Maybe if you proclaim it then you don't need to do something about it?) And on the other side, I have no doubt that gender exists. And also that we cannot will ourselves out of seeing it. What is fascinating is that, at the same time while listening to these "statements", I have kept on having experiences that again and again have to do with gender at an institutional level".

One could say that these writings were my way of making sense of these conflicting experiences and discourses, but this would only be part of the story. The other part started years ago. It is related to silence.

There are silences that are beautiful and desired pockets of rest and contemplation. And then there are the other ones; the loud, chaotic, troubled. Some silences shout. These silences dominate the many occasions when to speak feels inappropriate, or rude, or hopeless, or too complicated to even start trying. And there are also all those other times when thoughts and feelings cannot be delivered in a series of logical argumentative statements. Instead, they appear as a landscape of disintegrated signs that cannot be spoken because we experience situations we cannot make sense of. This book became a space where I could give expression to an accumulation of silences of this type.

The result is a series of reflections that combine literary, biographical, and philosophical perspectives. They are the creative act of imagining and playing with the word, the concept, and the being of *man* from the perspective of a subject who has always identified as woman. They were written in the space of a year, most of them unrelated to each other. I did begin to structure this messy collection and to create well-defined sub-sections with titles such as 'body' or 'experience' or 'sign', but I abandoned it. It felt useless, something that defeated the purpose of the free space that I so desperately needed at the time. Instead what you can read here are fragmented thoughts and images presented in one single flow.

Thank you for reading.

I AM MAN

I am man. I am kind of man. I am mankind. And can I get some help here … here as "in this body"?

•••

Have you ever thought that you could leave yourself, a percentage, somewhere after your body was gone? I would be in this room having a conversation with you and then leave, but not take the whole of me, only most of it. I could leave there a piece, lend it to you for a while, let it rest, exiled from this body (the one with this hair and this skin, and this age, and this sex). I would leave micro pieces of me in each one of the leaves of the trees, which look over the lakes. For an hour or two, they could rest there, moving with the wind, and without any hurry, follow me later and join me at the office; once they had been replenished, full of light.

In one of the evaluations of a course I taught a student wrote 'I wish to put Ana into my pocket and carry her around'. That was a weird comment, or so I thought then. But now I understand differently. (S)he got the idea of what I am trying to say here. I could let some part of me be in other people's pockets, be carried around, and take some part of you in my bag, hidden in my sleeve. That would help me to do man right, place some part of me in that guy running and that other one waiting at the cafeteria, rest for a couple of minutes in the chin of Bjarke when he shaves and feel the sharpness of the blade, take a nap on my father's shoulder. But I am contained, shaped; the whole of me is with me all the time, separated by this bodily filter. Like the photographic paper separates me from the beloved persons in the image. This body shape, this biological mass and all the multitudes of movements and change that happen here without me knowing; this is me, so contained and so foreign; a stranger in my own country.

I am this transported, heated, nervous vase with a liquid that would like to poor out, flow in thousand rivers, arrive to thousand seas. And it can't; instead it is sealed like an amphora containing a wine that can be imagined but can not be shared, not even by me. There are classical warnings about this kind of thought. Do not negotiate bodily sections, it is a bad bargain, no sharing of pounds of meat without blood; the pocket of my student would end up dripping; a nasty business. Maybe we need to die to finally spread in pieces arriving to a million destinations. Have you ever thought that another could be left to you, a percentage, somewhere after her body was gone?

•••

You have to sit close in this office. It is intimate, but we are not, and she says what I have heard three times already these past months: "I do not see gender", and I smile. She could have said I do not fear or I am never jealous and I would also smile because she strikes me as a lovely person, someone I could be friends with. She barely knows me, but she does not see my gender, she tells me. She is honest, and I wonder if she barely sees anything else about me. And I wonder if I barely see anything else about her. I do not need to believe her to trust her.

•••

The Main Hall is the opposite of an office; a void. Intimacy is an obscenity here; we know this and at Christmas parties we have to make this space disappear into darkness. But now there is light everywhere, this is another kind of celebration and I am listening to Lotte's farewell speech at a distance:

"And when I had my job interview for Head of Department the President told me 'You get the job because you are the best one, not because you are a woman'."

Ha ha ha ... people laugh, because man laughs at this kind of comment. We do man so well.

"You get the job because you are the best one, not because you are a man".

Ha – ha.

•••

Awake but before disclosing to the world that I have awoken is the best time to be man. I am still not in my form and I can barely feel my feet.

•••

Dancing will be a problem. I cannot be man while dancing. I have tried. The closest I can come to it is jumping up and down at a crowded concert, but otherwise it doesn't work. I need to drown into self-oblivion while dancing, become one with the beat. When I drown into myself I cannot find the man in there.

•••

'

I could do Tomas. Tomas will work for me. Not his love for crazy reality shows though, that will have to go, but I could metamorphose into him. Tomas cross dresses on very special occasions, and life is more fun with a red lipstick. He is like sunshine someone told him once. Tomas loves another man. Tomas loves me. His desire is like a familiar blanket. Once I told him that I surely had something androgynous about me, maybe I was like a man? And he could not stop laughing, "that was absurd, I was so feminine" he said. Tomas and I joke that we were one in a past life. We joke but we believe it.

•••

At 8 months pregnant with my son Anton, I am man, also chromosome wise.

•••

## QUEERING MY FATHER

The man in me is not hidden but here outside for everybody to see. Like in the seminar on the purloined letter of Lacan[2]. *The Purloined Letter* is a detective story of Edgar Allan Poe. In this story there is a letter addressed to the King which contains a secret that can incriminate the Queen. The Prime Minister notices this and steals the letter. During the second part of the story, both the police and the detective are looking for this letter to safeguard the Queen's reputation. The police think what most people will generally think, that the Prime Minister must have hidden the stolen letter in some secret place (Lacan will call this position 'realist imbecility', the gaze that believes we have direct unmediated access to the world, and therefore is blind. The thought of this makes me smile). The detective of the story discovers that the letter had always been outside, and that the Prime Minister had displayed it on the table of his cabinet for everybody to see. The man in me is like this letter, right here on display. My hands are my father's hands, a minor copy of the original version. Sometimes I decorate them with nail polish and large rings. My hands and I are having a drag party while the man in them smiles ironically at the theatrical performance. My son Kristian has my hands. Does he know that they are the woman in him?

•••

"Somewhere, on the edge of consciousness, there is what I call a mythical norm, which each of us within our heart knows: 'that is not me.'[3] "

Being a man is like moon landing. I would like it to be like the little prince in his planet, with the sensitive rose and his beautiful royal blue coat. Instead here I need to get the oxygen from an artificial system, a heavy one that I carry around. I am protected from sensing the outside by a thick inflatable material and see everything through a glass.

Girls never know, girls never know how do boys feel – sings Franz Ferdinand.

I am supposed to be here leaving my mark, a step, in this man moon but the only thing I can smell is my own skin inside the space dress.

•••

## MAN AND YOU

It's very easy to talk about Man and very difficult, impossible nearly, to talk about You.

I am naked of knowledge talking about You and worry that, although I have seen them ten thousand days, I won't remember the exact place of the moles of your back once You are not here anymore.

And I worry that although I carried you in my womb I can already not describe the exact combination of browns and greens in your eyes.

And I am lost wondering where will I go to visit your lively laughter.

And still when I talk about Man, because that's what I know how to do, I talk about You all the time...And it's impossible.

So I talk to You.

I talk to You about Man.

Maybe the problem of the way we write is that we write for Man about Man instead of writing to You about Us.

•••

"Reason is upset by gender. Reason aims at the unconditioned whole, the absolute of a phenomena". This expression is from Joan Copjec [4], but I could have taken this from Jürgen Habermas; of his vision of a reflective and moral dialogue spiraling upwards towards a consensual universalizing whole. The concept of man in its universalizing aim was to be a reflection of the triumph of reason, and instead it became the example of this eternal failing. We are a species with a wish doomed to fail. In the religious act of the Eucharist, in the consecration of the wine, the priest pours some water into the wine as a reminder of the humanity in God. The woman included in the universalizing man is like the drop of water; a daily existential reminder of our incapacity to be whole, to be godlike, and also a reminder that any God is worthless without an admiring spectator.

•••

Uffe, the external examiner, says he is sorry. It was meant as a personal email, he says. Didn't I notice the quotation marks in his sentences? It was not—Ana you are a visual experience. It was in quotation marks: "you are a visual experience". I am rewriting the email in my head, on repeat:

Dear Michael,
This was a very good examination. "You are godlike beautiful and a visual experience".
Kindest regards,
Uffe

I am hysterically laughing at the thought of this.

Do you know how the body arches in hysteria? I learned that from the sculptures of Louise Bourgois. It looks like a body captured in a scream. When the chest can't breathe anymore in one's being, it reaches out claiming the heavens. The arch of hysteria resembles a quotation mark.

•••

## REFLECTIONS ON THE SIGN, OR LACAN HAS TROUBLE UNDERSTANDING BEYONCÉ: IMAGINING A CONVERSATION BETWEEN LACAN AND THE ART OF PIPILOTTI RIST

The body lies down and looks up to the signifying chain of words and their linked concepts passing by, like clouds and birds on a summer morning. The word "man" and its many meanings. The body knows it is the space nurturing the skies and the winds. Storm Warning!

Your body always speaks the first words of the sentence...and the last ones.

Kiss, menstruation, smile, man: Your body speaks the word much better and with much more precision than your mind ever will.

A body can be whatever. The word man (or woman) gets anxious and a little bit jealous about this.

"Man" can mean whatever, but it doesn't mean the body will welcome whatever meaning home.

The body is the referent of a sign that denies being one.

The body is a referent that talks back, it bites back and makes the sign bleed. It is referent and sign (the signifier-the word-and the ideas/concepts the word refers to) in one. There is a shadow of pink in the blood.

When someone says that you are language structure, the body laughs, but also feels a little bit of pity for us humans.

•••

Deconstructing man is easy. It only takes paraphrasing the deconstruction of woman by Judith Butler: The
category of "men" is normative and exclusionary and
invoked with the unmarked dimensions of class and ra-
cial privilege intact. In other words, the insistence upon
the coherence and unity of men has effectively refused the
multiplicity of culture, social and political intersections in
which the concrete array of "men" are constructed. [5]

•••

## ICARUS

Now that we have just deconstructed man, re-construct-
ing it is not that easy, and still I can't stop myself, nor me
and nor can anyone. Man will not rest in the deconstructed
word–emptied; instead it will push forward to catch the
next meaning, wider maybe, more fluid maybe, but still a
meaning after all. The signifying drive is hungry. It will
push forward for the new signified to appear. Each word is
an impatient question mark in bold demanding its answer.

If you believe Lacan, subconsciousness is language, a system of signs related to each other through differentiation.
All identity signs joining the party and keeping each other at arm's length while looking for what is that you are
that is not me. What is it that nature is that is not man?
What is it that animal is that is not man? What is it that
woman is that is not man? Signifiers looking for differentiation to be able to signify something, whatever, anything
at all; looking for some anchoring. Identity words reach
out for new heights only to fly and fall again, and fly and
fall again, in an eternal movement doomed to fail to catch
a final signification. Whenever we try to express, to pro-
vide meaning, there is a wind, a sense of being out of tact,
a micro gap. We keep on throwing anchors in an ocean
of clouds.

•••

And then there are the ironic universals: "It is a truth universally acknowledged, that a single man in possession of a good fortune must be in want of a wife." [6] The first sentences of Pride and Prejudice of Jane Austen. Isn't it fascinating that, with this single sentence, we know that exactly the contrary is the truth of the society and time Jane Austen lived in? How brilliant of her to let us know a universal truth in reverse: "it is a truth universally acknowledged that a single woman without fortune must be in want of a husband." How a whole novel lays bare in one sentence, the drama of a whole life structured around such a mirrored universal scheme. Often the universally acknowledged meaning of a word is an ironic universal; it says more about its opposite than about itself. Is man that, an ironic universal?

•••

Our gender is a palimpsest
Not only of our lives but of the many lives before us.

Like cellular tattoos
We keep on writing with determination our own versions
of the gospel of truth
And the texts awaken here and there from their centennial
dreams and surprise us in the middle of a sentence.
Sometimes with a watery maaaaaaannnn

Who do you think you are? They ask, slowly stretching out
as the smile of the Cheshire cat

•••

## A ROOM OF ONE'S OWN [7]

Absolute power is to have the key to the door of one room; the only key of the only door. And then declare that you have it. Shout it within, filling each micro cavity in your lungs. Whisper it inside the palm of your hand, blow the words into your hair: I-have-the-only-key-of-the-only-door. All the freedom of the world is in that room; the hot sand and the shadow of your trees. Others know this. Let them whine and bank, bribe and plea. Hang the golden key on your lashes...blink, blink. "My room is no man's land" - paint each word with the tip of your tongue and taste its sweetness. In the middle of multitudes, the latest dinner with friends, the boring meeting, whenever, enter and close behind you.

•••

## IT'S WHAT'S INSIDE THAT MATTERS

I love my Sunday morning readings at the kitchen table. The day is still free of the melancholy that always dawns on Sunday's afternoon. I receive a very special gift, every Sunday morning, the thoughts and images that Maria Popova composes for her beautiful blog "Brainpickings". There is one that, while thinking about 'being man', comes back to me: Ursula Le Guin's reflections about herself [8]:

"That's who I am. I am the generic he, as in, "If anybody needs an abortion he will have to go to another state," or "A writer knows which side his bread is buttered on." That's me, the writer, him. I am a man. Not maybe a first-rate man. I'm perfectly willing to admit that I may be in fact a kind of second-rate or imitation man, a Pretend-a-Him. As a him, I am to a genuine male him as a microwaved fish stick is to a whole grilled Chinook salmon. […] I admit it, I am actually a very poor imitation or substitute man, and you could see it when I tried to wear those army surplus clothes with ammunition pockets that were trendy and I looked like a hen in a pillowcase. I am shaped wrong. People are supposed to be lean. You can't be too thin, everybody says so, especially anorexics. People are supposed to be lean and taut, because that's how men generally are, lean and taut, or anyhow that's how a lot of men start out and some of them even stay that way. And men are people, people are men, that has been well established, and so people, real people, the right kind of people, are lean. But I'm really lousy at being people, because I'm not lean at all but sort of podgy, with actual fat places. I am untaut."

And Ursula continues her reflection looking at who did man right. Hemingway, of course. He with "the beard and the guns and the wives and the little short sentences."

Hemingway - the archetype of genuine manness - and then I remember.

The memory that has appeared so clearly in my mind is an old photo; two children with dresses, femenine dresses, one of these children is Ernest Hemingway. Hemingway's mother dressed him and his older sister as twin girls. She was following the fashion of the times, but hundred years later Hemingway appears to us as a Pretend-a-Her. Is that what it takes? A firsthand knowledge of the superiority of the superficial, of the details; silk, laze, frills; to have experienced how a simple piece of clothing can change your identity. (Oscar Wilde would object. He would say that your identity is too humble a word, that clothing can change your life.)

9

'It's what's inside that matters.' That is a very instagram-able maxim, but most of us who have been on planet earth lately know otherwise. Men do not do dresses, and people, real people, the right kind of people, are supposed to be lean.

•••

## TAKE THE BRAINS BABE!

Woody Allen, who seems nearly as poor at being a first-rate man as Ursula Le Guin, would agree with her diagnostic on who did man right. Hemingway, of course, and Bogart – he will add – do not forget Bogart. He, who could embody Rich Blaine in *Casablanca* with the long silences, the strong sacrificial determination, and the impossibility to enjoy love. He, who made the best personification of Philip Marlowe. For manness, besides the guns and the short sentences of Hemingway, you need to throw in lonely evenings with whiskey and stoic suffering, one trench coat or two, and stir.

I wonder if Bogart as in Marlowe and Bogart as in Blaine are one and the same character – "the man". The only thing changing is that the female counterpart for Marlowe is the femme-fatale and for Blaine it is the femme-angelical. To do womanness, would Ilsa (Ingrid Bergman) with her sweetness, naivety, and devotion be the best councillor or should we turn to Vivian Rutledge (Lauren Bacall) in *The Big Sleep*[10]?

The James Bond movies know that we are automatically turned on by this dilemma. There we get the two-in-one version of things: the bad girl and the good girl in one single movie ticket. I wanted to be the bad girl. The bad girl was the brainy independent one. Between brains and virtue - take the brains babe! How could it be otherwise? A pity that death has always been the price to pay, but better a quick violent death than death by boredom. Now that I have decided that I can be man, I can choose James. He has licence to enjoy without capital punishment.

Agatha Christie, seldom welcomed in high culture canons, is so refreshing by comparison. In her novels women are wicked characters that seem one thing and are the other, complex psychological creatures with messy pasts and unmanageable desires. Humans who can poison, and plan, and love, and lie, and sacrifice ...women who can do the whole lot. No wonder, then, that she had to make her male detective an asexual character. Someone who could take that much womanness around him without falling apart; a brain with a moustache; Hercule Poirot, a man with plenty of grey cells and zero sexual liquids.

People have written articles about the male gaze that dominates the detective film genre; the masculine gaze, they call it. Women portrayed as devils or angels. I am not so sure about this. What made them think that the feminine gaze would look at it in a different way, that women could look at themselves, their sisters and daughters as something different than vamps and Madonnas. When there is only one keyhole different people end up gazing the same.

•••

## AND THE WORD BECAME SHADOW

Holding to words that separate me and humanize me
I am holding to words, embracing them and then pushing
them away

We become self and human by the word, by the possibility
that the word gives us to question, reveal, and disguise what
we are. The word is a gate to freedom
and also a chain, a categorical box; the past and the future
of our species dragging you down and along.

The imagination of other words that I can be frees me
I am stone
I am bird
I am your coffee
I am man
I am pizza (I wrote this one after it was revealed to me in
a dream like God was revealed to the prophets)

The imagination of other words that I can be separates
me of myself and throws me into a universal other. These
words make me company, like my thousand shadows
during the day, sewed with a thread of light to my bodily
presence. They nest unconsciously there as a possibility that may appear only under the right light conditions.

Peter Pan has a shadow who is free, who is a self, a 'who',
one that can rebel and move away and demand 'let me be!'

Peter Pan has still the wild uncontained imagination of childhood; the imagination of the night where darkness makes all and everything one and possible, where the shadow is king. Adulthood gives us power over our shadow. It owns our shadow like an identity that obeys our comings and goings.

I long for all the shadows of what could be and become, flying around me, playfully, like a breeze on a sunny morning, without asking from me any commitment, happy with having a life of their own.

Is there a Peter Pan syndrome for middle-aged women? Maybe that is impossible if you bleed, if you carry another human being forming inside you, a pregnant Peter Pan.

Pregnant, that is a word that will hold your shadow in place. There is something ironic about the destiny-like quality of this word ' pregnant'
You can't be pregnant and not be pregnant
It is not like
You can be an adult and not be an adult
You can't be pregnant and be a pizza ... or a man ... or can you?

The other shadows of the words of your being, the ones that could depict you, can't hold their space beside 'pregnant'.

Maybe they can't either when encountered with the word 'in love'. You can't be in love and not be in love.

Some words burn themselves in you in such a way that they melt the shadow into flesh.

•••

## A TRUTHFUL QUESTION

Sometimes it happens.
Sometimes somebody hands you a present unexpectedly,
across the table.

She is over 50. She wears golden eye shadow.
I realize I loved that, but only now, when remembering
her pose, the tone of her voice - a master class in how to
speak about truth.

It started as most banal conversations do when sitting
at a party table with strangers. I do not remember who
brought up the theme of children. Maybe it was us. It was
early September and talking about the summer holidays
of our respective families seemed such an easy topic.
How ridiculous! ... I know. I know by now that there are
no easy topics. Heartbreak can be waiting just around the
corner of any banal sentence.

When did she know? I ask her. She is looking straight at
me when she replies. "She was nine. One evening she
asked me, 'Mum, is there a vaccine so that a boy can become a girl and a girl can become a boy?'"

A simple chain of words carrying the revolutionary power of a historical event; the falling of the Bastille; 9/11;
moon landing. Our best and most eternal human stories
have been built on this realization. The atomic power of
a few words: 'I love you' 'I do not love you' 'I am not who

I am'. Nothing is the same ever again; not your past, present or future. Maybe nothing 'is' ever again.

I read once that beautiful questions allow for beautiful ways of looking at the world. I believe that. What about truthful questions?

In the days after, I held that present as something sacred and felt a sense of shame rising in me. Here, in this collection of "I am man" stories, I am playing poetically to be a man; to imagine the 'manness' in me. This is not a game of mirrors for children that believe in magic and are only nine. For a mother that has to answer to a son that is a daughter.

•••

## MOONOPAUSE

I will soon stop bleeding. My menstruations are so irregular now that it cannot take many more months (God of the hormonal universes, please don't make it be years!). I am in a state called perimenopause. This is a waiting hall to what? It is not adulthood anymore, more something like death. Lately the bleeding has been like a flood depleting me of energy. My uterus knows that this is its last chance, and it is not going down without a proper show. Meanwhile, I have become an impatient theatre director who can't wait to pull the curtain and send everybody home.

Menopause is a galaxy door transforming me from moon to sun; a bleedless me leaving behind the cyclical rhythms of my body: ovulation – increase – bleed – decrease - and repeat. I fail to remember what was it like not to bleed, what my child body felt like. I wonder if my menopausical self would allow me to feel more like a man; to get familiar with the experience of a body without moon phases, in a constant. I wonder what that constant will be; full moon, new moon, old moon, flat moon? Now that the biological dance of moods and fertility will not be here to remind me that I am flesh and not spirit, I need to find new ways to anchor my soul in my body. Dear men, send your anchoring tips my way.

•••

## PLEASE

Whenever I say moon, sea, sun, sand, stone, tree, body, door, blood, love, envy, music (oh music!), I sense gender. All these genderless English words are woven with the feminine and masculine cosmologies of my mother tongue Spanish. Latin languages gender anything that exists or can be imagined into feminine and masculine categories. All numbers are masculine (el uno, el dos...) and grouped numbers are feminine (la decena, la centena, ...) until they are not (el millar). And the 'no' is 'el no' (a he) and negation is 'la negación' (a she). All verbs (infinitives) used in their name form are masculine (el reir, el llorar, el dormir – to laugh, to cry, to sleep). Man is *el hombre* (a universal he); mankind is *la humanidad* (a universal she). The moon and her allure, the sand and her warmth, the tree and his shadow, the body and his movement. Sometimes my linguistic gendered universes feel so harmonic; envy is a she and so are blood and face, and fear is a he and so are bone and arm. Other times my words repulse their gendered roots as if they were dysfunctional transplanted organs. My body cannot be a he, or can it?

Once in a diary entry I wrote:

"I didn't know I could be so detached. I did not know my body would feel this way, because this was my body speaking. And I let her speak to myself. 'Here I am protecting you my love', she said and covered my shoulders with a blanket of mild distance."

I wrote that but it was a difficult negotiation – "please," I asked, "let him speak to me as a she, I need this today, I am exhausted". I am writing and reading those words, "Here I am protecting you my love, she said," and at the same time my mind sings its masculine echo – "Here I am protecting you my love, he said." *El cuerpo* is allowing me to write a feminine body in that memory, but it is not abandoning the room. It sits in the corner, patiently knowing that he will have the last word at my death bed, after my literary extravagances have abandoned me, when he will close my eyes and exhale my last breath. My body is and will ever be my 'he'.

•••

Mona Lisa: I am thinking "I am man". You should try.

Me: Me?

Mona Lisa: Yes, you. You standing there at the back. Try it. It is easy. It will make you smile.

Me: Maybe … maybe later. I cannot think while you are staring at me.

11

## BEGINNINGS

I entered motherhood by moving out of myself.

I can see the posture, my body heavily strange, immense, and ripe with the being of Kristian. I cannot stand straight; my hands, both of them on the wall, hold me up.

This pain expands from within and washes over me in waves pushing my consciousness towards the white hospital ceiling. My body knows and I do not, and I am leaving.

The rest of the room has dissolved into nothingness and Bjarke's hand is reaching out and anchoring me in the now. He does not know that I, the Ana that I could remember, is no longer here.

That night I was supposed to rest. You do that; try to sleep after your body has manifested as a volcanic eruption of life liquids, disposable organs, and the most tender human being; after you have abandoned yourself and become others.

I walk my body of soft wavy empty flesh to your side, Kristian, hurting in places that I did not know were me. I sit down, bowing my head to see your little face through the transparent plastic of the cradle.

I see you, my love.

This wave that hits me now doesn't push me away, but holds me tight, pulls me down, moves with your breathing, expands a smile of warmth inside me.

You began me as mother. We began you as a man. A history of manhood of thousands of years pulses between my motherly gaze and you; a history that will take you away from yourself into others and others into you.

•••

Soccer mum is now a stereotype; read "old cheerleader who is also good at making sandwiches".

My daughter was a good soccer player. If you love soccer and not only pretend to then you do man better.

Being that weird mum reading books during trainings and matches, I was failing quite miserably at stereotype embodiment. During those reading hours I would stop noticing the kicking and shouting in the background. I was far away being the man in my book.

•••

## MAKE YOUR AUDIENCE VISIBLE OR IT WILL CONTROL YOU

Tell me something,
What is in the mind of those that write on man?

Seven billion people
Their father
Their friends
Their lovers
Someone like me?

•••

Sitting for hours inside is the worst. I am outside on the terrace during the coffee break talking to Ben about research. I have moved our chairs to the only spot where there is direct sunlight. And David passes by and looks at us and then looks at me, up and down, without stopping to look me in the eye. He twists his head and gives Ben a canny smile and an appreciative look. Ben smiles back, a smile that exudes self-irony. I am not smiling, but nobody notices. I was never invited into smiling; that was a space that said 'men only'. David has passed and where were we? I cannot find my way back to our conversation. Somebody told me that gender does not exist. I hear you and I do not believe you.

•••

I want to change identity and name every now and then. Three years will be an appropriate period I think, not too long and not too short. If I could change that, would my belief system change too? Maybe I could provoke a form of name-induced amnesia, like being born anew to the world. Then I would also change my whole wardrobe. My man name should arrive with the wardrobe of the movie *A Single Man* or anything Yves Saint Laurent ever wore. Maybe the man name does not work if my shape does not change too. Maybe my beliefs are trapped exactly in the 30 centimetres of the curve of my hip.

•••

I have been and am passionately in love with men, with a man. The poet and philosopher John O'Donohue, in his book about beauty, explains how "many of the most intimate presences in our lives dwell within us in the form of thoughts. Though you might live with the one you love, he remains only physically adjacent to you; however, the thought of him can enter into the centre of you and become as intimate to you as yourself"[12]. He is so right and so wrong. Man dwells in me in the form of thought, but what is that thought if not so often (mostly?) the thought of his multiple forms?

•••

We can fail in our intent of a male-wholeness by quoting Joan Copjec[13]: "No man can boast that he embodies this thing—masculinity- any more than any concept can be said to embody being. All pretensions of masculinity are, then, sheer imposture; just as every display of femininity is sheer masquerade. A universe of men and women is inconceivable; one category does not complete the other, make up for what is lacking in the other. […] Rather than defining a universe of men that is complemented by a universe of women, Lacan defines man as the *prohibition* against constructing a universe and woman as the *impossibility* of doing so. The sexual relation fails for two reasons: it is impossible and it is prohibited. Put these two failures together and you will never come up with a whole."

So who are you and who would you like to be: prohibition or impossibility?

•••

Reconstructing man is not that easy. We can try by paraphrasing the claiming of difference by Audre Lorde
made to all women, now made to man, because for you
too—"the future of our earth may depend on the ability
of all women [and men] to identify and develop new definitions of power and relating across difference. The old
definitions have not served us, nor the earth that supports
us. The old patterns, no matter how cleverly rearranged to
imitate progress, still condemn us to cosmetically altered
repetitions of the same old exchanges, the same old guilt,
hatred, recrimination, lamentation and suspicion. For we
have, built into all of us, old blueprints of expectation and
response, old structures of oppression, and these must be
altered at the same time as we alter the living conditions
which are a result of those structures"…"we have chosen
each other/at the end of each other's battles/the war is
the same" [14]

•••

There is a machine at the fitness center that allows you to hang upside down. It is meant to have another purpose, though, helping you train different muscles, but hanging there without moving is a much more fascinating exercise.

The lycra bodies around me are now walking or running on what seems the roof of the room; the movements are strangely alien, the bodies acquire weird shapes.

I come to think that man depends. It depends on how I look at it.

I think we should have such a "hanging upside down machine" at the office, right beside the coffee machine; at all offices, beside all coffee machines. Then we could hang there changing perspective for a few minutes every day.

•••

## ROMEO

The signifier woman can't hold to it.

Her signified has become a rebellious teenager. She is expanding, slamming doors and shouting out loud. When the rage subsides, she is full on avoidance, not responding, hiding in secret silences. It's been going on for decades now.

Who is this? the woman signifier used to think. I gave birth to you and is this the way you treat me?

But the signified is not yet ready to feel any pity -
*I'm fed up, fed up, fed up... LET ME BE! GO AWAY! I'm moving out, do you hear me, I'm moving out!!!*

By now the woman signifier is so tired of this fight that she has given up. She takes the day off, lying on the beach, feeling the freedom of not caring anymore, finally.

The man signifier is looking at this show in horror. Take control of your signified, woman! What are you waiting for?...what a spectacle...you should be ashamed...discipline, ladies, discipline!

He sleeps well at night, reads the classics, and closes all the doors. And yet this morning, only for a few seconds, he thought he could remember a dream - the feeling of waves touching his bare feet, the heat, an anxious pleasure. Now it was forgotten, but it wasn't gone. Like worrying about a window left open by mistake.

Little does he know that there is no Juliet without Romeo. His signified learned it from her, to kiss, to say no, and then to say - *no, this is not me*. They sleep together under the stars making plans for other futures and other lands; whispering into each other's ears after having made love.

The man's signified doesn't dare to disrupt the rightful sleep of his signifier, he will do it peacefully, without the shouting; leave through the window, early at dawn, to never return to the mansion of manhood.

•••

## FOREIGN DESIRES

In thousand ancient languages
I am spoken.
Bittersweet whispering
warms me.

By thousand foreigners
for thousand years
I am traveled.
Their restless, estranged
DNA revived and electroshocked
by banal events that can kill
or bite a piece of your heart.

If I could make sense of it
the beat of their song,
heavy,
between my lips
and my breathing.

If I had received the dictionary of wishes
together with my hands
and my sex.
Somewhere where to look.
Something with bold capital letters,
where I would read about me, you, man and maybe,
and rest in revelation
holding words as truth.

But this can't be, my child
You will learn to be traveled by these ancient wishes,
stop asking questions,
comfort them with tea and the bread that your father
brought home this morning,
and they will not ask for sacrifices,
cut your insides out of exhaustion.

You will understand, my love.
They are tired of these long roads.
Lend them your bed,
kiss them softly,
hold them tight,
and they will fill you with the fire of thousand passions for
a thousand winter nights.

•••

If I have to be in a man I want to be in his tears

of joy
of love
of abandonment
of exhaustion

I want to be in the tears he could not hold back.

•••

Can you find pride in a woman's obsessive desire for a man?

There is a moment in Chris Kraus'[15] fictional memoir *I Love Dick* when the female protagonist asks if heterosexual women can ever declare pride in their sexual desire as we have seen in LGBT movements. Something about women's liberation gets messy and paradoxical when entangled with heterosexual women's desire of (the) man; when he is the one to be owned, imagined, eaten, seduced, used, projected upon, infatuated about.

•••

## PATRIARCHY IS FAKE NEWS

The President of the United States, Donald Trump, signed today an executive order by which all men will be called women and all women will be called men.

16

•••

## LA LUNA

Spanish genders everything that exists. It personifies all creation; like blowing humanity into each atom across the universe. It splits everything into the galaxies of feminine and masculine, but also it dissolves the dichotomy in a thousand mirror pieces by incorporating into it all what is and will ever be, your dreams and dark matter. When you learn other languages in the sense of langues of Lacan (the parole of Saussure) they manifest primordial language, that ancient ability of our species that tastes of water and fire and reincarnates everyone that ever was in everyone that would ever be in an ancestral dance structuring our very sense of self, our consciousness. It is like Siri Hustvedt explains in her book about time and future – all language links you to humanity. It is a collective.

Lacan, and before him structuralism, thought that 'langues' rested in language (the generic sign system with rules and grammar), and I have come to believe that with these two lovers things are the other way around. Language sleeps peacefully in the arms of your langue(s). Sometimes this loving bed is a threesome ... a foursome... a polyamorous garden. Your collection of 'langues' will pollinate each other and fight for priority, inseminating language into you in different ways depending on which one entered you first, depending on the one that you did not collect or learn in school but made you from within, turning your primordial crying and gazing into words. In which one did you say 'I' and 'you' and 'no' first? That primary langue is one with your neurons and cells and breath and the very structure of your liveliness. Edward Said said that his whole life, whenever he would speak aloud in English, he would always hear the same thought in Arabic, like an echo in his head simultaneously. I speak three languages on a daily basis, English, Danish, and Spanish. English and Danish, with their gender neutral articles and pronouns (it /a /the / en / et / den / det…), recreate a non-human non-gendered universe of nouns. The moon (Månen in Danish) is neutral. Us, the Latin gendered dichotomized structured babies, can understand Federico García Lorca when he says

en el aire conmovido
mueve la luna sus brazos
y enseña, lúbrica y pura
sus senos de duro estaño

in the stirred wind
the moon moves her arms
and reveals wet and pure
her bosom of hard pewter

we had dreamt of her bosom already when listening to her name.
la luna.

•••

## ON-OFF

Esther Perel[17], in her book about erotic intelligence, asks What turns you on? What awakens your desire?

Now I will leave this here with you for a while:

What turns you on?

Some reading experiences are the on-off desire version of things.
Some reading experiences are the on-off gender version of things.

It is summer and I am reading *Letters to a Young Poet* by Rilke[18]. I can taste its sweetness. Flying through the pages of this beautiful book, I am the young poet of mankind receiving the advice of Rilke about life and art, disappointment and courage. I am that man. Until the page where Rilke says in a confessional tone - with women, you know, it is different. They are different. Click!

Off man – On woman

Ah, how naive!
I was reading the book as if it was addressed to me, the reader. As if I could receive its inheritance. As if its golden message about being a poet could cross the times and the oceans, and nest in my heart. But no, with women, you know - Rilke knows, it seems - It is different.

Some (most?) think that the past cannot be changed. Well, they are wrong. When you are turned off from mankind and on into womanhood your past reading is changed forever. You are no longer in the position of the generic other; the audience; the universal reader. Now you are the one glancing through the window at the man-mankind-reader's conversation with the writer; like Andersen's little match girl, feeling how warm and luxurious the living room looks when seen from the outside.

I have turned the page. Click! I am now woman, the different one, suddenly transformed into a spectator looking at how Rilke advises young male poets about art.

The café-latte tastes like hot velvet, and I am passing on the pages of a book of Nietzsche. He philosophizes up and down, far and near, about the meaning of man. I listen to his sentences in my head, and smile at his electric passion and courage. He preaches about me, me-the reader, me—mankind; about my being, my destiny and my fears.

Until the page that turns me off. And Nietzsche [19] says in a rebellious angry tone - with women, you know, it is different. They are different. Click!

Off man – On woman

Shouldn't I have known this already, would you ask. One time naive, two times stupid, three times … ?

In the on-off gender game of reading, you are first everybody, that is to say man, and then you are woman. The transformation does not happen gradually. Like lightning, it strikes you on a random page. There. Where you did not expect it.

"Woman is ..." "Women are ..." They write, lightly; detaching half of mankind from whatever was said in all the pages before that. All those other pages that were about what really mattered - the meaning of heaven and hell, and life and death, and man and animal.

This is the on-off bottom of things. Now you are light and now you are darkness. Now you have sound and now you don't. Only that when it has happened there is no way back.

I wish it could be like the play-pause button on electric objects. You were something and then for a while you are paused and then you are again. But sorry, that is not the way this works. You were and now you are not because now you are woman.

On-Off

This – the classical heritage of human thought - was never intended for me. How could I ever have imagined that? Shouldn't I have known this already, would you ask. One time naive, two times stupid, three times ... ?

Esther Perel asks, What turns you on?
Now I will leave this here with you for awhile:

Man-Woman

•••

ENOUGH

You have to understand that it is exhausting, although I know, I know, they mean well. But try to imagine, you, man, to be

The other one
Exclusionary
Not existing
Cyborg-like
Phenomenal [20]

When all you ever wanted was to be.

•••

## ONE [21]

Be still and know that I am woman
Be still and know that I am
Be still and know
Be still
Be

Be still and know that I am man
Be still and know that I am
Be still and know
Be still
Be

•••

Deep attention to anything or anyone will dissipate any categorization into an abyss

or into God

•••

## ENDNOTES

1   This introductory quote is taken from the beautiful blog of Maria Popova "Brainpickings". It is from her essay titled *Ursula K. Le Guin on Art, Storytelling, and the Power of Language to Transform and Redeem*, January 30, 2018, which can be accessed here: https://www. brainpickings.org/2018/01/30/ursula-k-le-guin-walking-on-the-water/.

2   This reflection was inspired by Homer, S. (2005). Jacques Lacan. Abingdon: Routledge; Lacan, J. (1989 [1966]). *Écrits: a selection*. Abingdon: Routledge.

3   This quote is from Audre Lorde in her collection of essays Lorde, A. (2017). *Your Silence will not protect you*. London: Silver Press, page 96.

4   The quote of Joan Copjec is from Copjec, J. (2015). *Read my desire: Lacan against the historicists*. Brooklyn, NY: Verso, page 219.

5   The quote that I am paraphrasing here is from Judith Butler in Butler, J. (1999). *Gender trouble: Feminism and the subversion of identity*. New York: Routledge, page 14.

6   Austen, J. (2009 [1813]). *Pride and Prejudice*. London: Penguin Books.

7   For this reflection I was inspired by the book of Virginia Woolf (2018 [1929]). *A room of one's own*. London: Vintage.

8   The quotes of Ursula K. Le Guin on the text titled "It's what's inside that matters" are from

Le Guin's essay "Introducing Myself," which appears in Popova's blog "Ursula K. Le Guin on Being a Man" October 17, 2014. This can be accessed here: https://www.brainpickings.org/2014/10/17/ursula-k-le-guin-gender/

9    Image: Ernest Hemingway and her twin sister in (EHPH-SB1-SB1) A Record of Ernest Miller Hemingway's Baby Days, Book I: From birth to 23 months old. pag. 96. The John F. Kennedy Presidential Library and Museum. Retrieved from https://www.jfklibrary.org/sites/default/files/2018-07/EHScrapbook1.pdf

10   Images: (To the left) Humphrey Bogart and Lauren Bacall from the 1946 film The Big Sleep, 1946. National Motion Picture Council. Retrieved from https://commons.wikimedia.org/wiki/File:Bogart_and_Bacall_The_Big_Sleep.jpg

(To the right) Promotional still of Humphrey Bogart and Ingrid Bergman in American romance film Casablanca, 1942. No copyright notice. Retrieved from https://commons.wikimedia.org/wiki/File:Humphrey_Bogart_Ingrid_Bergman_Casablanca_Promo_Still.jpg

11   Image: Portrait of Lisa Gherardini, wife of Francesco del Giocondo; Monna Lisa, la Gioconda or la Joconde, by Leonardo da Vinci, 1503–1519. The Louvre Museum, Paris Image

retrieved from http://cartelen.louvre.fr/cartelen/
visite?srv=car_not&idNotice=14153

12  This quote is from John O'Donohue's from his book
O'Donohue, J. (2003) *Divine beauty: The invisible embrace*.
London: Bantam, page 44.

13  The italics in the quote of Joan Copjec are my own.
It is from Copjec, J. (2015). *Read my desire: Lacan against
the historicists*. Brooklyn, NY: Verso, pages. 234-235.

14  This quote is from Audre Lorde from her collection
of essays, Lorde, A. (2017) *Your silence will not protect you*,
London: Silver Press, page 105.

15  Chris Kraus (2017). I love Dick. Electronic book.
Copenhagen: Gyldendal.

16  Image: President Donald J. Trump in the Treaty Room
at the White House, Monday January 22, 2018, in
Washington, D.C. (Official White House Photo by
Joyce N. Boghosian). Retrieved from https://www.
whitehouse.gov/briefings-statements/photo-president-
donald-j-trump-signing-h-r-195-federal-register-
printing-savings-act-2017/?utm_source=link

17  Perel, E. (2006). *Mating in captivity: Unlocking erotic
intelligence*. New York, NY: Harper.

18  Rilke, J. M. R. (2012[1903]). *Letters to a young poet*.
Electronic edition. Start Publishing LLC.

19  Nietzsche, F. (2013). *Afgudernes tusmørke*. Translated by
Peter Thielst. Copenhagen: Det lille Forlag.

20  Woman seems to always need an adjective in order
to be: The other one, in Simone de Beauvoir;
Exclusionary, in Judith Butler; Not existing,
in Jacques Lacan; Cyborg-like in Haraway;
Phenomenal in Maya Angelou.

21 Inspired by the beautiful psalm of the Bible "Be still and know that I am God", which I learned from listening to the mystic meditations of James Finley in the podcast "Turning to the Mystics with James Finley" of the Center for Action and Contemplation.

## ACKNOWLEDGMENTS

I wish to thank: The first readers of this book, Cathrine Bjørnholt Michaelsen and Elaine Yang for their comments and generous support, Tomas Pernecky for his inspiration and encouragement, Adam Doering for his healing kindness and integrity. Kellee Caton for her copy editing and joyful love. Adriana Budeanu for her sisterly love. Claudia Eger and Amira Benali for their honesty and enthusiastic support of my creative writing. Mia Larson and Catheryn Khoo-Lattimore for their friendship and care. My husband, Bjarke Møller, for his unwavering love, passion and encouragement. To my family for the joy and boundless acceptance.

## I AM MAN

Ana María Munar is a gender scholar and Associate Professor at Copenhagen Business School, Denmark. She has written extensively on gender, feminism, and philosophical perspectives on diversity and equity. Her latest work studies the nature of desire. Born in Spain, a passionate lover of the Mediterranean and of the arts, she lives between Copenhagen and Mallorca.